# CONTENTS

## A NEW SOURCE OF EVIDENCE FOR USE IN RE

■ Evidence about religious belief and practice enters classrooms in a number of ways. Many schools own or have access to artefact collections, for instance. Many schools give students the opportunity of experiencing first-hand a visit to a place of worship and of seeing acts of worship taking place in various community settings. Many schools explore students' personal experience in relation to some of the moments and events in human life that are reflected in different ways in the world's major religions. The *Faith and Commitment* series adds an extra dimension to the range of evidence available to students by presenting as directly as possible the personal ideas and experiences of people who belong to faith communities.

*Faith and Commitment* has been created to support work in Religious Education with students from Year 9 upwards. Although it does contain factual information on religious beliefs and practices, it is not designed to be or intended for use as a series of textbooks or as a free-standing course in secondary-phase RE. Instead, it offers a range of primary evidence which teachers and students can continually draw on to enrich their existing work in RE.

The format of *Faith and Commitment* is important. Apart from FACT-FINDER panels, which appear where we feel a student may need access to information explaining a particular term or reference or giving further research leads, the text of the Students' Books has been provided not by us but by the responses of interviewees to our questioning. The experiences, ideas and opinions and the words used to convey them are theirs. Our only intervention – apart from extracting the essence of the interviews from the tapes – has been to devise a framework of themes within which the interviews, then the books, then teaching and learning based on using the books, could be organized. This was done before interviewing began. The interview extracts appearing in the books have undergone only 'cosmetic' editing: that is, mainly the insertion of punctuation and conjuctions or, occasionally, reordering of phrases to improve readability.

Interviews were carried out solely for the purposes of creating the *Faith and Commitment* books. Interviewees were briefed at the outset about the audience they were talking to and some of the ways in which their interviews in printed form might be used. Communities saw typescripts and had the freedom to ask for changes. Few requests were made. The interview extracts therefore represent the sorts of answers that people from faith and denominational communities might give if invited into your classroom to talk with students about aspects of their religious life, minus the formality that would be likely to surround such an event and potentially inhibit the sharing of ideas. Since we talked to about ten people from each community, their interviews offer a broad range of perspectives.

Visitors to the classroom might be expected to bring with them things which illustrate what they want to say or give their meaning extra clarity or depth. The people interviewed for *Faith and Commitment* were asked if they could show us items from their personal and religious lives that are especially important to them. Most did, and many of the artefacts you see on the pages of the *Faith and Commitment* books represent these items or were generously lent to us by the interviewees so that we could photograph them. Some items were so significant that they became the focus of a whole interview answer. Interviewees were also asked about any important visual images that they carry around in their minds. There is no single section in the books for their answers to this question, but wherever possible we have tried to reconstruct photographically the ideas that were described to us and include them on the same page as a relevant extract from another part of the interview. So in terms of both words and images, the books in the *Faith and Commitment* series convey strong and unique impressions of personal religious lives and individual spirituality.

Using primary evidence in RE leads to first-hand learner responses and encounters which can have outcomes less predictable than those which come from using, say, the programmed factual content of a textbook. Unlike a textbook, though, primary evidence can also lead to insights and discoveries of great significance to learners – and, where the evidence is as accessible as a religious or personal artefact, to learners of any age. The content of *Faith and Commitment* is intended to operate on the sort of level and in a similar way to the sort of stimulus that an artefact can provide. However, there are obviously limitations to its use. One is imposed by the medium of words. Teachers must make judgements about the language abilities of their student groups and individual students before selecting extracts to use from *Faith and Commitment*. In making their selection, they should bear in mind that the interviewees in the books, like their students, demonstrate a range of practical language skills. Also, there is no direct correlation between language level and length of extract, many of the longer passages being in a simple narrative style.

Another limitation lies in the intellectual and emotional maturity of students, individually and in groups. At Year 9 through to Year 11, this aspect of student development varies tremendously between individuals, across groups and from school to school, where it can be strongly affected by local conditions. Any advice or grading of extracts in the *Faith and Commitment* series by us according to suitability to levels of student ability or maturity would be generalized and unhelpful. Like assessments made about the appropriateness of any task or resource in relation to a particular teaching situation, this is a matter best left to the individual teacher on the spot.

What this Teacher's Manual does offer is an overview of some of the teaching and learning opportunities which the *Faith and Commitment* series can support and promote, including:

- A review of current issues in and requirements of schools in providing Religious Education, collective worship and appropriate conditions for the spiritual, moral, social and cultural development of students. This is the shared background to the development of the *Faith and Commitment* materials and their effective use in schools. (See pages 13 to 18.)

- Profiles of six classroom activities trialled in schools using the first five Students' Books in the *Faith and Commitment* series, indicating teaching objectives, learning outcomes and showing a range of evidence of achievement. These cover RE in Years 8 to 13, both general RE across the full ability-range and GCSE and A-level examination groups. (See pages 25 to 39.)

- Suggestions for further activities and approaches. Some are familiar but with a new focus, others are made possible by the existence of material of the content and format of *Faith and Commitment*. (See pages 19 to 24.)

- A survey of some of the cross-curricular opportunities which a resource like *Faith and Commitment* can help access. (See page 23.)

- An analysis of the content of the first five Students' Books in the *Faith and Commitment* series. This is intended as a practical aid to integrating the material into existing schemes of work. (See pages 40 to 55.)

This Teacher's Manual approaches its task on the assumption that colleagues teaching RE at Key Stages 3 and 4 already use a range of teaching strategies and approaches. It also assumes that RE departments have the multifaith knowledge skills both to support their students in appropriate ways across the full range of expectations that their locally agreed RE syllabus has of this age-group and to support any non-specialist teachers who may be involved in the delivery of the subject. It is the use of *Faith and Commitment* in this professional context which the Teacher's Manual is concerned with. This means, for instance, that information for teachers about the faiths encountered is limited to explaining a few specific elements in the background to the local faith communities which we feel teachers may need to understand in order to be fully prepared for using the material.

For similar reasons, we have decided not to offer a list of additional resources. *Faith and Commitment* is intended to be a flexible resource which can be integrated with a wide range of approaches, programmes of study and teaching materials. We expect colleagues to want to make for themselves any links between *Faith and Commitment* and other resources for RE on the basis of what they consider suitable and compatible with their own teaching preferences and their students' learning needs.

## THE INTERVIEWS

■ In selecting communities and people to be the focus of the *Faith and Commitment* books, we applied several loose criteria. Chiefly, we wanted the communities to be properly representative of their own faith tradition and the people to demonstrate a spread of the ages, roles and circumstances that make up a balanced community mix, such as parent, child, grandparent, priest, community worker, lay official. We also wanted the cross-section of people to reflect a social profile that most students would recognize as familiar, whether they have any practising faith background or not. This meant finding interviewees who would fit a Key Stage 3 or 4 student's description of being like them or their family, or like their friends, or like people where they live, or like people they know.

Communities tended to select themselves on the basis of factors like their size, history and prominence. This took us to the Shree Sanatan Mandir in

Leicester, for instance, which is one of the largest and longest-established Hindu temples in Britain. It also took us to the New Testament Assembly church in Tooting, which is headquarters for the New Testament Assembly worldwide. We felt it was important to get as close as possible to the mainstream of each tradition featured in the *Faith and Commitment* books.

The people who were interviewed either volunteered to take part or were chosen by their communities, in both cases in response to our overall list of the family roles, age-range and religious roles that we wanted to see reflected. We did not think it appropriate to conduct interviews on any other basis, although self-selection did skew our aim of trying to achieve a 'typical' social profile. For instance, quite a few interviewees from all communities have higher than average academic qualifications. However, one thing that *Faith and Commitment* does very effectively is to question whether a concept like 'typical' has any value or meaning when it comes to matters of personal experience and religious understanding. This is important. Every interviewee has their own unique terms of reference and in most cases it is these which give the interviews their relevance to the books in which they appear.

Interviewees were encouraged to describe their ideas, attitudes and views from a personal perspective. This means that personal opinions and interpretations are frequently expressed. In most cases, this is evident from the form of words used, but teachers may want to remind their students that this is the case. Interviews clearly distinguish between individual responses in the first person singular and generalized comments in the first or third person plural. However, some students may be susceptible to the impression that anything which appears in print is unarguable. Interviewees were not invited to be spokespeople on behalf of their communities or of their faith, nor would they or their communities have wanted this to be the case.

All participating faith communities scrutinized typescripts of the interview extracts we selected for publication. Few alterations were made, and these were mainly to clarify meaning. No extreme views are expressed.

In most cases, faith communities also saw and sometimes contributed to the FACT-FINDERS which appear alongside the interviews. FACT-FINDERS are there to ensure that students have access to the technical content of the interviews; their job is strictly limited to this one function. Interviewees were briefed to make allowance for an audience with a limited background knowledge of their faith tradition. In the event, the amount of technical content in interviews did not become an issue in the selection of extracts.

## THE COMMUNITIES

■ Although the interviewees were not acting as spokespeople for their communities, what emerges powerfully from the interviews in each Students' Book in the *Faith and Commitment* series is a sense of shared purpose, of belonging and of community. However, teachers should bear in mind that, just as individuals may belong to communities aspects of which they support and aspects of which they might challenge, individual communities and the groupings to which some belong are components in the larger picture of a particular faith tradition, always confirming its main focus but sometimes differing in their approach to it.

There is obviously a point in teaching and learning about faith traditions where generalization has to be left behind. There are no archetypes for believers, and assertions that Christians do this or Jews believe that are too easily made and too frequently flawed. One of the aims of *Faith and Commitment* is to present evidence about belief and practice in a form which allows students to begin appreciating its diversity for themselves when they are able and ready to do so. To assist this aim, and to help colleagues be alert to differences as well as commonalities within faith traditions, a short introduction to a distinctive aspect of each community featured in *Faith and Commitment* follows. Teachers may also wish to explore the denominational background to some of the communities for themselves.

## Parish of St Saviour's with St Mary's, Cotham, Bristol

Like a number of Anglican parishes, St Saviour's with St Mary's is an amalgamation brought about by recent demographic changes. Tony told us that amalgamation, which happened in 1976, caused 'a certain amount of subdued acrimony'. Roger, who was a parishioner at St Mary's before it closed, explained: 'We were very high and they were very low'. By 'high', Roger means High Church.

One of the guiding principles of the High Church movement, in which Anglo-Catholics are prominent, is that of the Real Presence of Christ in the Eucharist. This focus on the Eucharist and its celebration has had an important influence on the ritual and ceremony of the Anglican church. In the mid-nineteenth century, for instance, the Privy Council was hearing appeals against High Church vicars accused of re-introducing pre-Reformation customs and practices. One was allowed to keep the crosses he had installed in his church provided they were not placed on the altar. Another was told it was illegal for a parish priest to wear a chasuble. The Vicar of St Paul's in Knightsbridge almost caused riots by placing lighted candles on the altar and appearing in a surplice (instead of a black gown) with a surpliced choir.

A lot of what is now accepted as 'traditional' Anglican ceremonial is relatively recent innovation. The Festival of Nine Lessons and Carols from King's College Chapel was introduced in 1918 by a dean strongly influenced by Anglo-Catholic styles of worship. What now seems alien is what was considered customary in the Anglican church in 1825, when the Bishop of Bath and Wells wrote to his clergy advising them that 'the Sacrament administered monthly would, believe me, produce a sensible amelioration in the feelings and habits of your parishioners'. Eucharist was then normally celebrated once a quarter.

Today, the distinction between 'high' and 'low' could seem a bit irrelevant to many members of the Cotham community. These two traditions amalgamated locally 'very, very amicably' according to Tony, and quite a long time ago. But there are still issues which can divide Anglicans. In the case of the ordination of women, some of the fault-lines surround High Church perceptions of Anglican identity and emphasis.

# New Testament Assembly, Tooting, South London

The New Testament Assembly is one of several prominent black churches in Britain, of which the largest are the Church of God of Prophecy and the New Testament Church of God. Established in Jamaica in 1954, the NTA reached Britain in 1961 and now has almost twenty churches nationally. There are also NTA churches in the U.S.A., Canada and Africa.

The NTA follows in the Pentecostal tradition of Christian faith. Key elements include accepting the Bible as the inspired word of God and belief that all have sinned, that repentant sinners are justified by faith alone, and that there will be a premillenial second coming of Christ.

Some interviewees refer to one or all of three stages in spiritual development which have special significance to Pentecostalism and to the beliefs of the New Testament Assembly. These are the stages of being 'born-again', being baptized and being baptized in the Holy Spirit (hence the term 'Pentecostal'). The following definitions are taken in full from the *New Testament Assembly Handbook*:

**New birth, regeneration, conversion, or born-again**. These terms are synonymous and they signify the process of being made a child of God, and joint-heir with Jesus Christ. It is wrought by the Holy Spirit in the sinner who believes in the atoning death of Christ.

**Water baptism**. Subsequent to the new birth, the believer *must* be baptized, i.e. immersion in the water in the Name of the Father, the Name of the Son, and the Name of the Holy Ghost. This is an outward testimony to the believer's inward change, and a sign of the believer's death to sin and resurrection with the Lord Jesus Christ.

**Sanctification**. This is the process of being made clean and set apart for God's purpose. Sanctification, therefore, begins at regeneration. There are three phases to sanctification:
  - By faith in the atoning death of Jesus Christ, the Holy Spirit cleanses the believer from all unrighteousness.
  - The believer is sanctified by taking heed to the Word of God.
  - Being set apart for special service.

**Baptism with the Holy Spirit**. Baptism with the Holy Spirit is a special endowment of power for service upon the believer. Speaking in languages unknown to oneself, as the Spirit gives utterance, is the initial evidence of this experience.

Jesus, before he ascended, spoke to His disciples and commanded them to go to the Upper Room at Jerusalem and there wait for the promise of the Father. The disciples obeyed and on the day of Pentecost the Holy Spirit came upon the whole body of believers present.

This phenomenon marked a new dimension in their Christian experience. This was demonstrated in Peter's first post-resurrection message which brought about one of the greatest revivals, and marked the beginning of a new era, according to the New Testament Scriptures. It is therefore important for all believers to seek this experience, 'for the promise is unto you and to your children and to all that are afar off, even as many as the Lord our God shall call.' Believers should not only seek to be initially filled with the Spirit but should endeavour to retain the Holy Spirit in their lives.

Interviewees also talk about the importance of the NTA's National Convention. In the *New Testament Assembly Handbook*, this is described as the organization's 'yearly Spiritual Feast'.

## Archdiocese of Liverpool

The interviewees in *Committed to Christianity: A Roman Catholic Community* belong to three different types of Roman Catholic community within the Archdiocese of Liverpool: a Roman Catholic high school, a parish and a prayer group. The interviewees' various parishes provide them with a neighbourhood focus for their faith. The school and the prayer group in different ways offer additional dimensions to expressing shared religious identity, and these are also explored.

Of these communities, the prayer group has a significance which needs to be put into its context in contemporary Roman Catholicism. This is how Father Des described his first contact with his local prayer group:

> Three of us priests used to pray together on a Sunday evening to support one another. When we were down to two, because one went to Latin America, we started watching Esther Rantzen on *That's Life!* instead. So we decided to go to a local prayer group once a month for support, and we got more and more involved.

> Very often, the Catholic community is accused of maintaining structures but forgetting about the Kingdom. Our prayer group is about building the Kingdom not only in structures but in individuals. It's not just personal renewal for its own sake that we're concerned with. We encourage people who've been supported in this way to go back to their parish communities and offer service there.

The word 'renewal' is important here. This is a prayer group committed to spiritual revival, a process very much at the heart of the Charismatic Renewal movement in the Roman Catholic church and strongly associated with prayer groups. Father Des refers to his discovery of Charismatic Renewal as his special moment (see *A Roman Catholic Community*, pages 34 to 35). The accompanying FACT-FINDER explains where the word 'charismatic' comes from and what it means in this context. Pinning down its meaning is important as 'charismatic' is a term which is often used more loosely.

Some commentators describe the charismatic movement generally (it can be found in nearly all Protestant denominations as well as in the Roman Catholic and Eastern Orthodox churches) as 'neo-Pentecostal'. Certainly, Pentecostalism gained a high public profile in the United States in the Fifties through the work of prominent preachers like Oral Roberts, and this may have led Christians from other traditions to look at how they expressed their faith. Whatever its precise origins, a definable charismatic movement could be identified across Christianity by the end of the Sixties.

Charismatic influence has arguably gone on to have its greatest impact on the Roman Catholic church, where it now has important supporters. As Father Des explained:

> Certainly, one of the things we can say is that Charismatic Renewal is not just on the margins. The World Committee for Charismatic Renewal in the Catholic church has its headquarters in Rome. Both Pope Paul XI and Pope John Paul II have said, 'This is at the heart of the church.'

> Locally, I would say that it would be seen as involving just a few people. But in the archdiocese, when we hold a big Day of Renewal, we get two or three hundred people. And they're just the very committed ones. When Cardinal Suenes came to Southport a few years ago, we had over a thousand people at the celebration of Mass, people who knew of his support for Charismatic Renewal.

## Shree Sanatan Mandir, Leicester

Hinduism offers such a range of religious experience and practice that focusing on what individuals believe is an essential stage in trying to build a larger picture.

In India, the religious life of a Hindu person is shaped by many factors. Geography is important. Not only do religious traditions vary from region to region, there is bound to be an influence on personal belief if, for instance, a Hindu lives in the part of Northern India where Krishna and Rama lived. Language as a religious medium is also important. Some of the more recent religious literature is written in vernacular languages, not Sanskrit, and this tends to localize it. For example, the *Hanuman Calisa* is a popular text written in Hindi and mainly recited in Northern India, where Hindi is spoken. Additionally, different areas show variations in ritual or in the pantheon which is revered or in temple architecture and practice. Some festivals, like Holi in Northern India or Ganesha Chaturthi in Maharashtra or Durga Puja in Bengal, are forms of religious expression which have developed a particular regional significance. A person's age, sex and caste also have an impact on belief. As Dhanlaxmi says in one extract from her interview, 'Brahmin people are particularly attached to Lord Shiva. Women also have a special affection for Shiva.' And, as well as responding to circumstances, Hindus also have the opportunity to make choices between devotional and philosophical approaches.

It is this diversity which Ramanbhai is referring to when he describes Hinduism as 'a liberal religion'. India has given Hindu diversity its context, and there is no easy substitute for it. Supporting Hinduism in Britain via a network of less than a hundred temples is challenging. As Narnarayam admits, 'A lot of people come to this temple and there's a range of different ideas and thinking … people come up to us with religious questions because we're Brahmin. And we have to answer them.'

The Hindus who worship at the Shree Sanatan Mandir are mainly either from the Indian state of Gujarat or descended from Gujarati families. This means that they benefit from sharing a common regional Indian language and culture as well as a similar experience of Hinduism. Gujaratis have a long history as seafaring merchants and traders.

# United Synagogue, Hendon, North London

'United Synagogue' is the name of a long-established federation of Jewish synagogues in Britain. The families which it serves are Ashkenazi Jews of the Orthodox branch of Judaism. In *Committed to Judaism: A Jewish Community*, several interviewees make strong statements not only about what Jewishness means to them but about how their concept of Jewish identity stands in relation to those of Jewish people from other branches of Judaism.

Jewish people come from two major cultural streams. Ashkenazi Jews are from northern and eastern Europe (*Ashkenaz* denotes an area which approximates to northern France and Germany); most Jews living in North America are descended from Ashkenazi families. Sefardi Jews are from the Mediterranean rim and Arab countries (*Sefarad* means the Iberian peninsula, and many Sefardi Jews are descended from exiles from the Spanish Inquisition). As a result of their cultural differences, Ashkenazi and Sefardi Jews tend to form separate communities.

Cutting across the cultural streams are several branches of Judaism distinguished from each other by differences in belief and/or practice and/or attitudes to the modern world. Eddie, in his interview (see *A Jewish Community*, page 24), talks about 'far right' and 'centrist' Judaism to identify some of these differences.

The main branches of Judaism began to emerge in response to the challenges for Jewish people which came with the changing social climate in some parts of Europe during the Age of Enlightenment in the eighteenth century. In an attempt to prevent assimilation of Jews into mainstream European society resulting in religious apathy or even conversion, Reform Judaism (also called Liberal or Progressive Judaism) began and continues to adapt Jewish religious belief and practice to contemporary thought and society. Orthodox and Conservative Judaism responded in differing ways to the same challenge with greater emphasis on preserving Jewish religious tradition. Orthodox, Conservative and Reform Judaism remain conscious of the spiritual and cultural challenges of the modern world in which they exist. To ultra-orthodox and traditional forms of Judaism, the modern world is not a factor to which concessions are considered necessary.

Within the branches of Judaism which have synagogues as a focus for religious activity and across the cultural streams are the congregations. There are a number of Jewish congregations in Britain, including the United Synagogue, the Spanish and Portuguese Jews' Congregation, the Federation of Synagogues, the Union of Orthodox Hebrew Congregations, the Reform Synagogue of Great Britain and the Union of Liberal and Progressive Synagogues. There are also some Independent Congregations.

Orthodox Judaism includes the belief that the Torah is 'given from Heaven', that the halakhah (religious law) derives directly or indirectly from an act of revelation and that Jews are required to live in accordance with the halakhah as interpreted by rabbinic authority.

# RESPONDING TO DEVELOPMENTS IN RE

The books in the *Faith and Commitment* series acknowledge and in their approach respond to the changing curriculum framework and the changing expectations of schools within which RE teaching and learning is now taking place. *Faith and Commitment* has set itself the objective of being flexible enough not only to resource RE but also to support some of the other elements in the development of students at Key Stages 3 and 4, such as their social, cultural, spiritual and moral awareness and understanding, to which RE teaching is expected to make a contribution. With careful preparation, the material also has a part to play in collective worship (see page 18).

**MORE TIME FOR RE**

■ As well as reaffirming the statutory place in school life given to RE by the 1944 Education Act, the 1988 Education Reform Act has extended it. Section 8 of the Act now makes it compulsory for maintained schools to provide RE for all pupils. This means RE in Years 12 and 13 for schools with sixth forms. It also means a new approach for schools which have previously been delivering RE to Years 10 and 11 in an indirect form or for only some pupils via examination classes.

In *The National Curriculum and Its Assessment: Final Report by Sir Ron Dearing* (December 1993), assumptions are made that RE will receive 45 hours a year of curriculum time at Key Stage 3 and 5% of total curriculum time at Key Stage 4. The SCAA *Model Syllabuses for Religious Education Consultation Document* (January 1994) was developed on the basis that RE would receive a minimum of 45 hours a year at Key Stage 3 and 40 hours a year at Key Stage 4. The SCAA Model Syllabuses are of course non-statutory and intended as advice to Agreed Syllabus Conferences only.

**MORE SCOPE FOR RE**

■ Significantly, one of the first statements made in the 1988 Education Reform Act is a definition of curriculum as all those activities of schools designed to promote the 'spiritual, moral, cultural, mental and physical development of pupils' and their preparation for the 'opportunities, responsibilities and experiences of adult life and of society' (Section 1). Although these are not specifically the objectives of any one subject, and although there would be cause for concern should RE become a school's main means of delivering any one of them, in highlighting the importance of these particular aspects of student development the Act has set up requirements which are influencing how RE's contribution to school life is focused and measured.

In addition, Section 8 of the Act adds the qualification that RE should:

> reflect the fact that the religious traditions in Great Britain are in the main Christian whilst taking account of the teachings and practices of the other principal religions represented in Great Britain.

These two requirements have provided both the main statutory framework and the philosophical basis for the subsequent development of RE.

Although current locally agreed syllabuses for RE vary in their form and content, many now reflect widespread agreement about the aims and nature of RE. This has been helped by the recent pioneering work of research projects like *FARE* (Forms of Assessment in Religious Education) and *Assessing, Recording and Reporting RE*. In particular, syllabuses tend to identify two major dimensions to RE which echo and develop Sections 1 and 8 of the Education Reform Act:

(i) knowledge and understanding of Christianity and other major religious traditions represented in contemporary Britain and the ways in which they approach or explain some of the fundamental issues of life

(ii) assistance to pupils in their personal search for meaning and purpose in life through the exploration of human experiences which raise fundamental questions about beliefs and values

The first dimension is often referred to as 'explicit' RE. This combines the obviously religious – the practices, beliefs, history, language and places of worship of believers – with the personal experiences and intentions of believers that produce faith and commitment.

The second is 'implicit' or 'affective' RE. It deals with the whole range of experiences concerned with feelings, relationships, a sense of moral obligation, questions of judgement, the making sense of life's mysteries which have been part of the human search for meaning throughout history. They may not in themselves be religious but they often involve religious answers.

These dimensions continue to be restated. DFE Circular 1/94, *Religious Education and Collective Worship*, says that:

RE in schools should seek: to develop pupils' knowledge, understanding and awareness of Christianity, as the predominant religion in Great Britain, and the other religions represented in the country; to encourage respect for those holding different beliefs; and to promote pupils' spiritual, moral, cultural and mental development.

In defining the aims of RE, the groups working with SCAA on its *Model Syllabuses for Religious Education Consultation Document* (January 1994) agreed that:

Religious education should help pupils to:

• acquire and develop knowledge and understanding of Christianity and the other principal religions represented in Great Britain;

• develop an understanding of the influence of beliefs, values and traditions on individuals, communities, society and culture;

• develop the ability to make reasoned and informed judgements about religious and moral issues with reference to the teachings of the principal religions represented in Great Britain;

- enhance their own spiritual, moral, social and cultural development:

  - developing awareness of the fundamental questions of life raised by human experiences and how religious teachings relate to them;

  - responding to such questions in the light of their own experience and with reference to the teachings and practices of religions;

  - reflecting on their own beliefs, values and experiences in the light of their study.

- develop a positive attitude towards other people and their right to hold beliefs different from their own, and to living in a religiously diverse society.

The Consultation Document also offers two attainment targets – 'Learning about religion' and 'Learning from religion' – which match closely the dimensions to RE which locally agreed syllabuses are already expressing.

'Learning about religion' covers 'knowledge and understanding of the beliefs and practices of religions' including 'the main concepts, objects, places and people significant within each religion'. Also:

An important part of this area of attainment is the ability to understand and offer interpretations of symbols, religious objects, art, religious language and literature. Pupils should also be able to demonstrate knowledge and understanding of the fact that religions influence individual communities and societies, particularly concerning moral codes and ways of living.

'Learning from religion' takes account of the fact that 'evaluation of religious and moral issues arising from human experiences and from study is a long established area of attainment and one that is now incorporated in the General Criteria for GCSE Religious Studies'. It also acknowledges that 'there is significant support for the extension of this area of attainment to cover the more "affective" dimensions of the subject'. In addition:

The cognitive dimension [of this Attainment Target] enables pupils to learn from religion by discussing, responding to and evaluating a variety of views arising from the study of religion. The affective dimension ensures that pupils learn from religion by, for example, reflecting on the relevance of religions for their own lives.

| RE AND SPIRITUAL DEVELOPMENT |
| --- |

■ Spiritual development is central to RE, and much of the discussion about the RE curriculum, about RE programmes, pedagogy and learning experiences takes this for granted. However, it may be worth pausing to reflect on the spiritual dimension to RE in more detail.

Although RE is not the only part of school life which can be sampled for its contribution to students' spiritual development, OFSTED inspections nevertheless look for evidence in school that appropriate provision in this area is being made. A definition used by OFSTED in its *Framework for the Inspection of Schools* (1993) is that:

> spiritual development relates to that aspect of inner life through which pupils acquire insights into their personal existence which are of enduring worth. It is characterised by reflection, the attribution of meaning to experience, valuing a non-material dimension to life and intimations of an enduring reality.

Some locally agreed syllabuses include an attainment target specifically associated with student spiritual development. SCAA's *Model Syllabuses for Religious Education Consultation Document* (January 1994) does not do this on the grounds that 'to limit it to one AT would be to trivialise its importance'. However, it does identify some of the main aspects of spiritual development which might be included in locally agreed syllabuses. These are:

> **The development of beliefs** ... informed by the study of the teachings of Christianity and other religions and philosophies, developed through opportunities to discuss with others, and partly assessed through the ability to evaluate.

> **A sense of awe, wonder and mystery and feelings of transcendence** ... encouraged largely through the experiences to which pupils have access ... and developed through discussion with others.

> **The search for meaning and purpose** ... encouraged by giving pupils opportunities to ask questions, and informed through the study of religions. Ability to balance answers given to questions about meaning and purpose may be partly assessed through the pupil's ability to evaluate.

> **Creativity** Pupils should be given opportunities to express their innermost thoughts through a variety of media.

> **Feelings and emotions** Pupils should be encouraged to regard feelings and emotions as valid human responses, and should be presented with resources which evoke feelings as well as an intellectual appraisal. They should be encouraged to consider the balance between 'feeling' and thinking.

## RE AND QUALITY

■ In addition to responding to current curriculum debate, approaches to RE should take account of what constitutes effective teaching and learning in the subject.

This is what OFSTED's *Framework for the Inspection of Schools* (1993) offers as its criteria for assessing the quality of learning in RE:

> Good learning in religious education occurs when pupils gain an understanding that religion has practical application to everyday life. At best, pupils are helped to recognise that the scope of religious education is wider than knowledge of Christianity and other major religious traditions and that it relates those traditions to a broad experience of life. Those who have no background of religious faith

should come to recognise that religious beliefs can give guidance and motivation in ethical considerations, and that, to their holders, beliefs have an explanatory power which gives coherence and significance to aspects of life which might otherwise appear fragmentary and disconnected. Pupils should gain an increasing understanding of ways in which religion involves believers in corporate celebrations and in individual affirmations of their faith. They should be able to form their own views of religious issues, explore them openly, orally and in writing, and develop the maturity of their thinking and the skill with which they can analyse their own and others' beliefs.

In discussing the quality of teaching, the Framework suggests that 'teaching should make clear the relationship between religious belief and personal and social behaviour' and concludes:

Inspection should lead to a judgement of how effectively teachers have presented the range of complex concepts and material to their classes and how well they have succeeded in establishing regular occasions for reflection and the kinds of reading and discussion that engage and motivate all their pupils and enable them to develop a sense of morality as well as gaining factual knowledge.

## FAITH AND COMMITMENT AND RE

■ *Faith and Commitment* has approached from a practical position the development of a resource which is exciting and effective in meeting some of the requirements of RE now evolving in response to current thinking about curriculum, assessment and inspection.

In terms of content, *Faith and Commitment* is careful to present students with specifics rather than generalizations: real people belonging to actual local communities who are living out their faith according to an interpretation and valuation of its significance expressed in part through their personal responses and personal experience. It is a presentation which offers students the nearest printed equivalent to a dialogue with people in faith communities. Ideas are exchanged at a level which allows individual insights and students' own experience to be relevant and meaningful. Information about what religious communities do to celebrate their faith and venerate its significance – and *Faith and Commitment* encounters a wide range of forms of religious expression – is given additional value through students being given access to the personal perspectives of people for whom these things are a fundamental expression of belief.

In terms of teaching and learning, *Faith and Commitment* offers teachers and students opportunities rather than solutions. These are opportunities to do with acquiring knowledge as well as understanding, and developing skills as well as information and insights. Because the *Faith and Commitment* books are not reference books or textbooks, students are encouraged and will almost certainly at some points need to do additional research and investigation of their own. Conversely, *Faith and Commitment* can be used as a research source in itself.

Providing evidence without evaluation also creates a resource which supports student development in other ways, raising questions not just of information but of meaning, questions to which there may be no ready answers. This provides a useful stimulus both to reflection on some of the ideas and experiences described in the books and to thinking and talking about some of the significant feelings and experiences students may themselves have had. It is also a stimulus to discussion and exploration of the implications that significant ideas and experiences can have in terms of influencing how individuals and communities interact with the world around them.

An important feature of *Faith and Commitment* is that, although the project has always been conceived as one aimed at Years 9 to 11, the interviews have yielded books which naturally and comfortably present material suitable for a broad range of intellectual and operational abilities within Key Stages 3 and 4, as well as for different levels of spiritual awareness and emotional maturity. There is no correlation between the complexity of the feelings and experiences discussed and the complexity of the language used to express them, which means that some quite sophisticated ideas can be remarkably accessible. The material can be assessed and differentiated without difficulty according to ability, task or outcome as teachers feel appropriate. There is no upper age-limit on its applicability.

What ultimately distinguishes *Faith and Commitment* is the authenticity, honesty and directness of its approach and content. *Faith and Commitment* portrays people who believe, which is not the same as offering an analysis of the religions they believe in. If RE is part of a curriculum which traces its motivation back to promoting the development of students in spiritual, moral and cultural ways, then the word 'development' has to be operative. This is RE which needs to take account of students' growth as people, giving proper emphasis to helping them understand the world they are preparing to take part in. By offering a view of religion through the eyes of people to whom it has personal value, *Faith and Commitment* encourages students to form meaningful links in both cognitive and affective ways with the significance of religious expression and to begin to understand how and why it is that religion is a major dynamic in individual lives as well as in society as a whole.

## FAITH AND COMMITMENT AND COLLECTIVE WORSHIP

■ In its aims, and in arrangements made for providing it in some schools, there are clearly overlaps between collective worship and RE. DFE Circular 1/94, *Religious Education and Collective Worship*, identifies aims for RE which include providing students with opportunities 'to consider spiritual and moral issues and to explore their own beliefs'.

Further guidance in DFE Circular 1/94 also identifies areas where the meaning of collective worship overlaps with the content of *Faith and Commitment*. For instance, it 'must in some sense reflect something special or separate from ordinary school activities and it should be concerned with reverence or veneration paid to a divine being or power'.

*Faith and Commitment* was not created as a source for supporting collective worship in schools. However, some of the personal descriptions of religious experiences and attitudes included in the books may be suitable for use in secondary-school acts of collective worship.

# GETTING STARTED

There are several broad approaches to teaching and learning in RE which *Faith and Commitment* can support, and this section briefly indicates some of them.

However, the effective use of any resource depends on understanding where its potential lies, and this has implications for preparation and organization.

## THE MATERIAL

■ The main text of the *Faith and Commitment* Students' Books is made up of interview extracts grouped under seven thematic headings (listed on page 40). Apart from the logic of opening each book with a section called 'About Me' which introduces the interviewees, there is no significance in the order in which subsequent sections run. Likewise, the interview extracts within each section may be used in any order, although naturally occurring links between extracts have been taken into account in the way in which they are grouped within sections.

No assumptions have been made about how teachers and students will want to use the evidence that the *Faith and Commitment* books contain. Any interview extract and any illustration on any page is a self-contained point of focus which can be linked to other points of focus within the series or to other activities and materials. To allow this flexibility, the series is extensively indexed and cross-referenced. How this is done is explained in more detail on pages 40 to 41.

FACT-FINDER panels have been added to interview extracts to avoid leaving students stranded where an interviewee's 'own words' include religious language that may be unfamiliar. It is assumed that students have a minimum of knowledge of the faith in focus at their fingertips, however the FACT-FINDERS are not intended to provide all the detailed background information they might require. Brief explanations of words and phrases are given and/or the religious beliefs, practices or sacred texts to which they relate are indicated, so that students can research further factual details for themselves.

## TEACHING AND LEARNING

■ Because *Faith and Commitment* is an open-ended resource which can operate at a number of levels, teachers intending to use it must be clear about the learning activity they want it to support and its objectives.

Of course, any form of evidence used in any subject needs to be treated with care. Unlike didactic materials such as textbooks, evidence is capable of raising questions as well as suggesting answers. Used as a stimulus, it can lead learning activities in any number of directions. However, some of the extracts in *Faith and Commitment* have a powerful affective dimension. Others are provocative at an information level. To ensure that the open-endedness of *Faith and Commitment* leads to constructive and appropriate outcomes, we strongly advise colleagues to avoid using any extracts from *Faith and Commitment* with which they are not personally familiar.

Using evidence in RE leads to powerful direct learning experiences, but it does need a controlled environment in order to succeed, which may seem contradictory. Although students should be left to their own investigations and reflections and be allowed to draw their own conclusions from using material from the *Faith and Commitment* series, they may need explicit help in understanding what evidence is and how it differs from other sources of information they use.

To be effective, this type of evidence also needs to be introduced as part of an activity and in a learning atmosphere which encourages respect for it. Part of getting that atmosphere right is making sure that students have the right sort of conditions for the work they are doing. This can often simply be a matter of classroom organization. Activities aimed at getting students to reflect on personal experience may need an intimacy better suited to individual or paired work. Follow-up might be more appropriate in small groups than with the whole class. Providing sufficient access to the evidence is also important. A single book shared by a group of varying reading abilities is not likely to encourage respect for the evidence, nor is a confetti of poor photocopies. If access to the evidence is restricted by practical conditions, it may be better to limit the scope of learning activities accordingly.

As well as respecting the evidence, the learning situation should also respect the learner's ability to handle it, emotionally as well as intellectually. *Faith and Commitment* contains an extensive selection of material which in itself is widely differentiated according to linguistic and conceptual complexity, this being the nature of personal experiences described in the first person. However, to enable all learners to feel that they have found something meaningful in the evidence, tasks and outcomes associated with using it may also have to be differentiated.

Getting these conditions right applies to all the approaches which follow.

## PROVIDING STIMULUS

■ A framework of activities can be created around *Faith and Commitment* to provoke an initial response which provides starting-points to further activity. The initial response is likely to be a personal one. The further activity should aim to move students towards a more objective position where, for instance, they can consider their own experience in the light of other people's and begin thinking about aspects of human experience in relation to religious belief and/or forms of religious expression.

The framework of activities might be as follows. As individuals or pairs, students explore from their own experience one of the more general themes in the *Faith and Commitment* books – like 'What I Feel Strongly About', 'Where I Belong', 'Things I Find Challenging' – sharing and talking about their ideas in groups or as a whole class. They are then introduced to one of the titles from the *Faith and Commitment* series (not necessarily the same title for the whole class) and encounter interviewees' experiences relating to the theme chosen, with plenty of opportunities to discuss their discoveries and responses. Gradually the scope of the work expands so that for each student it begins, using other *Faith and Commitment* books, to take in evidence within the chosen theme from a range of religious traditions. Local programmes of study may influence which traditions these are, but there are advantages in preventing this stage of work becoming random by encouraging students to look at evidence across several Christian denominations and/or across the major world religions. Other sources of information and other approaches can now be brought in.

■ This could lead to a self-contained activity or be part of the strategy of a larger project, providing it with a starting-point, for instance, or adding a dimension to work in progress.

Reflective work needs a relatively tight focus to allow opportunities for meaningful contemplation. *Faith and Commitment* provides this in two forms: in interview extracts and in some of its more figurative illustrations.

Activity might be developed as follows. Keeping within a single theme to provide a common basis for subsequent discussion, students are given or select one extract to read and think about. Some interesting starting-points can be picked up if between them students are working from books reflecting a number of different faith traditions. They then write a response in whatever form they want to what they have read or talk about it in appropriately sized groups.

Alternatively, working in pairs or in small groups, students are given one of the figurative illustrations to look at and think about. They discuss what it means to them then possibly consider and talk about images from their own experience which are meaningful. Work might move on to start looking in a similar way at some of the more formalized religious images that also appear in the books or to consider the verbal images that the interviewees use to describe aspects of their experience.

■ The index to each *Faith and Commitment* Students' Book contains an average of 120 key words. These are the objective terms of reference that students would expect to see in any index, words like 'prayer', 'food' or 'families'. In many reference books, looking up these words gives access to equally objective information presented along the lines of 'This is what Jewish people do ...' or 'This is what Hindu people believe ...'. Generalization in most forms of information-giving is unavoidable. However, in the *Faith and Commitment* books, looking up a word from the index is almost certain to locate something quite different, a personal experience or opinion which needs to be thought about carefully before it starts to give up its meaning.

By being accessible as a source of research evidence, *Faith and Commitment* offers students opportunities to extend their study skills in parallel with work which is developing their religious understanding. These opportunities can be provided, for instance, as activities which put *Faith and Commitment* alongside reference and textbooks in RE as an information source. Using the indexes to *Faith and Commitment*, students can find and use quotations which relevantly explore personal feelings and attitudes associated with an aspect of religious expression – like sacred books, praise and worship, rites of passage or festivals – about which they are gathering information from a number of sources. The scale and timing of this type of work would depend on a school's programmes of study in RE. It might be an aspect of project work or give the focus to a single-session activity. It might be a way of starting a topic or equally a means of revising it.

The section FINDING YOUR WAY AROUND (pages 40 to 55) has an extensive content analysis of the first five Students' Books in the *Faith and Commitment* series according to references made to forms of religious expression.

## EXPLORING EMPATHY

■ When ideas associate with feelings, understanding another person's point of view involves more than just an intellectual response. The *Faith and Commitment* series contains a number of interview extracts likely to make a strong appeal to students' hearts as well as their heads. They provide interesting opportunities for teachers to explore with students how feelings differ from opinions and what both contribute to the way we try to understand other people's beliefs and attitudes and express our own.

Activity in this area is unlikely to succeed from students' first contact with the *Faith and Commitment* materials, and we do not recommend that *Faith and Commitment* is used for activities of this type without having first had a more explicit context established for its use. However, once that context has been established and students are working purposefully with *Faith and Commitment*, they could be asked, for instance, which interviewee they most identify with or which interview extract has had the most impact on them, with a discussion of why.

Because *Faith and Commitment* is based on conversations and because in conversation people say what they think *and* feel – it's much easier to write without emotion than to talk like that – interview extracts often contain emotions and opinions mixed together. Where teachers are encouraging students to start discriminating between different ways of expressing belief, activities might be developed using the section 'What I Feel Strongly About' to explore whether the 'feelings' expressed there are emotions or opinions. How can you tell? What effect does each have on the way we respond?

## LOOKING AT ISSUES

■ An area which the interviews in *Faith and Commitment* develop in different ways is the relationship between faith, values and morality. Interviewees frequently talk about what they believe and how it influences the values they hold. They also discuss how these convert into goals for and limits to their own personal behaviour.

Care should be taken with how the ideas of personal morality described in *Faith and Commitment* are introduced to students. Some interviewees have clear and unambiguous personal codes of conduct. Others struggle with putting their personal morality into practice. None intended that their values or codes of conduct should be held up as models.

Activity which looks at specific issues creates opportunities for exploring personal morality in terms of what motivates people's attitudes and actions. The specific issue could be chosen by the students or equally be suggested by one of the *Faith and Commitment* interview extracts. Students obviously need the chance to develop and discuss their own opinions as a starting-point. However, the focus could be on what students think have been the influences on the attitudes they express. Follow-up activities could widen the search for influence or guidance to include several faith perspectives. Using a range of pre-selected *Faith and Commitment* interviews, students could look for evidence of what the position of someone from the faith communities on the issue is or might be. The factors that led them to their conclusions could then be investigated.

■ Opportunities for using *Faith and Commitment* as a means of supporting other areas of the curriculum at Key Stages 3 and 4 – particularly those associated with the spiritual, moral, social and cultural development of pupils – are offered both in the form and in the content of the Students' Books.

The discrete interview extracts in the first person and range of styles of visual imagery in *Faith and Commitment* provide stimulus with the potential to support work in any subject area in which responsive or creative activities associated with exploring the human quest for meaning take place:

- In **English**, this can lead to responsive writing, responsive discussion with a partner, or creative writing. Activities using *Faith and Commitment* in English are being tested for *Faith and Commitment: Teacher's Manual 2*.

- In **Art**, interview extracts and the questions they raise can give starting-points to work exploring themes like 'Who Am I?'

The content of the *Faith and Commitment* books, which is analysed in detail in FINDING YOUR WAY AROUND (pages 40 to 55), provides more-explicit contributions to other subject areas:

- For **PSE**, interview extracts provide first-person discussion from a number of cultural perspectives of areas such as community, family, role, peer pressure, ethical issues, prejudice, and decision-making.

- For **History**, interviewees talk from their own cultural point of view about links between their personal identity and cultural tradition. Some traditions featured in *Faith and Commitment* have been involved in events which have contributed to shaping the twentieth century and its conscience.

- For **Geography**, interviews throw light on subjects such as social migration.

- For **Citizenship** and **Social Studies**, interviews give a multicultural perspective to topics such as rights and responsibilities, the role of the individual and the role of society, the family and belonging to a community.

■ Finally, the value of the *Faith and Commitment* books to teacher professional development in RE should not be underestimated. To experienced teachers of RE, the hard content of *Faith and Commitment* will be familiar although the form in which it is presented may be new. At completion, the series will present about one hundred interviews with people whose religious faith is the motive force in their lives. Few of us are ever likely in the normal course of our work to meet so many people from so many faith traditions under circumstances where conversation on such personal topics would be possible or appropriate. Indeed, many interviewees remarked that they rarely have conversations of such a penetrating type.

The perspectives and dimensions that this sort material can offer our own understanding of religion are significant. In particular, there are opportunities to remind ourselves through our own responses to the interview extracts in *Faith and Commitment* of what it is we are trying to help students appreciate in religion when we use words like 'affective'.

All of us carry round in our heads anecdotes and stories connected with religion which we use to illustrate our teaching. The memorable power of some of the *Faith and Commitment* stories is bound to add to many repertoires.

# SIX TESTED ACTIVITIES IN RE

The following activities were devised and tested by teachers during the piloting of *Faith and Commitment*. They demonstrate some of the ways in which the material can support teaching and learning in RE.

*Note* The examples of students' work are reproduced exactly as written by them except that we have corrected spelling mistakes where necessary.

## GROUP 1

**Group Description**
Year 8, mixed-ability RE set

**Theme**
Festivals in Christianity

**Teaching Objectives**
To investigate how Christian festivals are celebrated and what those festivals mean to believers

**Time Allowed**
One session of one hour

**Resources Used**
Paper for jotting
Paper for finished writing
*Committed to Christianity: An Anglican Community*, pages 24 to 30
*Committed to Christianity: A Pentecostal Community*, pages 28 to 31
*Committed to Christianity: A Roman Catholic Community*, pages 26 to 31
*Skills in Religious Studies, Book 1* (Mercier & Fageant, Heinemann)
Library resources from shelves

ACTIVITY

*Individually*, students jotted down what they thought a festival was.

*Whole group and teacher* brainstormed Christian festivals generally. Students wrote the names of festivals they knew on the board then came up with criteria for sorting them. Main festivals were identified. A question/answer session explored what students already knew, with teacher listing on the board information offered under headings like 'Ritual', 'Tradition', 'Symbolism', 'Who celebrates?', 'Where celebrated?'

*Group work* Teacher gave out *Committed to Christianity* books and identified an extract for each student to consider. Students worked in groups organized according to festival, with larger groups subdivided. Groups identified common factors, ideas and issues that emerged from their set of interview extracts. A spokesperson was briefed.

*Teacher* co-ordinated oral feedback on what groups had come up with.

*Whole group and teacher* discussed how these new findings related to students' original thoughts about festivals.

*Small groups* used *Committed to Christianity* books and textbook sources to look for common and recognizable elements in the different subjective and objective accounts of their Christian festival.

*Individually*, students wrote about how their interviewees' descriptions of their Christian festival related to other descriptions they had found.

## TEACHER'S COMMENTS

Plenty more room for manoeuvre and lots of opportunities for bringing in other material provided by the interviews in the *Faith and Commitment* books.

## GROUP 2

**Group Description**
Year 9, low-ability RE set

**Theme**
What I Feel Strongly About

**Teaching Objectives**
To give students opportunities to express what they feel strongly about, to consider what arouses those feelings and to put their responses into a broader context

**Time Allowed**
Two sessions of one hour each

**Resources Used**
Paper for jotting
Paper for finished writing
Paper for drawing
*Committed to Christianity: An Anglican Community*, pages 20 to 23
*Committed to Christianity: A Pentecostal Community*, pages 22 to 27
*Committed to Christianity: A Roman Catholic Community*, pages 21 to 25
*Committed to Hinduism: A Hindu Community*, pages 19 to 25
*Committed to Judaism: A Jewish Community*, pages 21 to 25

ACTIVITY

*Teacher stimulus* Unfinished sentences were written on the board: 'I feel that ...', 'I feel strongly ...'. Teacher verbally offered endings to the sentences, some light-hearted, some controversial, some food for thought.

*Whole group and teacher* Group reacted to teacher's statements and discussed them. Were some of the feelings described more 'important' than others? What does 'important' mean in relation to feelings?

*Individually*, students jotted down their own endings to the unfinished sentences.

*Whole group and teacher* shared ideas, looking at similarities and differences amongst the feelings expressed by the group.

*In small groups of two or three*, students were invited to consider pictures on specific pages in the *Faith and Commitment* books (see above), jotting down what the pictures suggested to them and any strong feelings which the pictures provoked.

*Whole group and teacher* discussed what the students found in the pictures. Teacher related these responses first to the students' earlier responses then to the interview extracts which appear with the pictures. Some interview extracts were read. Could students see any 'religion' involved?

*Individually* and silently, students reassessed in the light of what had passed since the activity began the meaning of the words 'What I Feel Strongly About'. They were invited to think carefully about what they really did feel strongly about, and to write about it or draw a picture of what came to mind.

*Whole group and teacher* shared ideas. Teacher read from and showed examples of students' work.

## TEACHER'S COMMENTS

Went like a dream. Amazed at the offerings that this 'low ability' group came up with. Some very mature and magical contributions, particularly to oral work.

### EXTRACTS FROM STUDENTS' WORK

I feel strongly that people shouldn't be bothered and picked on because they are different.

I feel strongly about the polluted seas.

I feel strongly that people should not beat and abuse people and adults.

I feel strongly that the law should not have a certain age for things.

I feel strongly that animal testing should be banned.

I feel strongly that if you become a parent you should look after your children.

I feel strongly that there should be basketball courts so kids aren't on the streets.

I feel strongly that people should not be racist.

## GROUP 3

**Group Description**
Year 9, top-ability RE set

**Theme**
Hindu Ideas of God

**Teaching Objectives**
To investigate the Hindu belief in one God in many forms

**Time Allowed**
One session of one hour

**Resources Used**
Paper for jotting
Selected passages from *Committed to Hinduism: A Hindu Community*
Teacher-created worksheets about and pictures of Hindu gods

ACTIVITY

*Whole group and teacher* Recap on previous work based on using the 'Dolphin' poster (a computer-generated, apparently abstract, pattern in which some people are able to see a three-dimensional image of a dolphin), going back over the range of responses it generated. Teacher drew conclusions from previous work which was then extended to considering belief in God.

*Looking and reading* Students used worksheets and pictures to form a preliminary view of what the Hindu idea of God might be.

*Whole group and teacher* Teacher read several prayers from *Committed to Hinduism: A Hindu Community* to introduce hard evidence of Hindu ideas of God: the Gayatri Mantra (page 41 – God as creator), the Brahmasabanta (page 43 – belonging to God; the separateness of the soul), and 'O God, lead me from untruth to truth ...' (page 40 – mortality, immortality and eternal life). Discussion explored concepts as they arose: reincarnation, God as creator, God as omniscient.

Links with Jewish, Christian and Muslim ideas of God were explored. How could all these different ideas of God add up?

Teacher read several more extracts from *Committed to Hinduism: A Hindu Community*: Deena's special moment (page 34), Deena's statement that 'Hinduism's just another path to God' (page 21) and 'CM's' comment that 'Some people think that Hindus are idol worshippers' (page 19) – to explore what worshipping God in many forms means to Hindus and how this form of religious expression can be misunderstood.

*Individually*, students wrote reflectively.

## TEACHER'S COMMENTS

This is a very good group which discusses well and thinks quite deeply, often coming up with unexpected ideas. The readings from the *Faith and Commitment* book worked extremely well to lead the students' thinking through the various concepts approached in the lesson and served as an excellent link with work done in the previous lesson. Aims were achieved and the target end-point in the lesson was reached.

### EXTRACTS FROM STUDENTS' REFLECTIVE WRITING

It doesn't matter how many 'idols' you have so long as it follows the rules of your particular religion.

I think religion is on its own road and God is in the centre of all the roads joining together.

God is a thought, not a sight.

I don't think it is wrong for Hindus to worship idols to get closer to God. They may believe that God made the idols they worship.

If people need some figure or idol to see and believe in, it tells me that they lack faith in their god.

I believe people have the right to worship what they want. I think a lot of people want to believe in God because they're told he's there, but they can't.

The question of whether there actually is a god is not an important one. The important question is whether you believe in god and what god means to you. I went to church for a long time before I started to realize how little god and Jesus meant to me. I realize I can work to better myself without the ideal of 'trying to be more like Jesus'.

Hindus have posters, models and paintings of their various gods but when they pray they're not praying to lumps of plastic or bits of card. God helps people cope with everyday life. With shrines and pictures, Hindus are not trying to replace him, they're simply getting closer to him.

It's up to the person whose religion it is to make up their own mind who and what they want to worship.

*cont.*

## EXTRACTS FROM STUDENTS' REFLECTIVE WRITING                *cont.*

Hindus praying to God through idols I think is wrong. I think you should pray straight to God and not use idols as messengers.

I think there is nothing wrong with praying to idols because I think people need to see what they're praying to. It gives them more belief in that god.

People need gods as something to put their faith into and believe in, probably in the same way that children need invisible friends.

God confuses me. Well, not God exactly, but religion. There's loads of religions that people follow, but they all end up at the same thing, a sort of ideal or a divine force.

## GROUP 4

**Group Description**
Year 10, GCSE Religious Studies set

**Theme**
Festivals in Three Religions

**Teaching Objectives**
To investigate the importance of festivals to believers

**Time Allowed**
One session of one hour

**Resources Used**
Paper for jotting
Graffiti sheets
Paper for finished writing
Paper for posters
*Committed to Christianity: A Roman Catholic Community*, pages 26 to 31
*Committed to Hinduism: A Hindu Community*, pages 26 to 33
*Committed to Judaism: A Jewish Community*, pages 26 to 33
Various library resources

ACTIVITY

*Students in pairs* drew up lists of festivals in one of the three religions of Christianity, Hinduism and Judaism. They then put facts to the festivals using a variety of sources.

*Individually* and in silence, students chose one festival each and wrote one or more thoughts about aspects which seemed most important to them.

*Whole group and teacher* in a feedback session compared results of silent writings.

*In three groups*, students read interview extracts about 'My Favourite Festival' from the three religions, listing on their graffiti sheets aspects of importance under headings such as 'People', 'Food', 'Actions', or using headings of their own. The lists were cross-referenced to the names of the interviewees and the results quantified.

*Whole group and teacher* Teacher gave more information about the interviewees. Whole group considered whether the important aspects they had identified on their graffiti sheets related to factors to do with the interviewees, such as their age or situation.

*Small groups* put together a statement about what they considered to be the most important factor in why festivals are enjoyed.

*Individually,* students wrote a GCSE-style evaluation based on the evidence researched in the lesson: 'Religious festivals can only be worthwhile if the meaning behind them is understood'.

## TEACHER'S COMMENTS

The lesson worked well, seemingly enjoyed by all of us. The students became very involved with reading and comparing their interview extracts, which meant that work carried over into part of the next lesson.

### SAMPLES OF STUDENTS' WORK

Many people think that celebrating religious festivals is very important and has great value. This is because it's a time of year when you think especially of what happened many years ago and celebrate it in the way of how it was – for example, eating foods either that have significance in how they are prepared or in the ingredients. Another example is the giving of presents, especially at Christmas-time, when people exchange gifts in remembrance of the wise men giving presents to Jesus at his birth.

People also use this time of celebration to relax and enjoy being with their families and friends and to have a good time. There is excitement and joy as people celebrate something that is of importance to them.

But is it really important to them? Sometimes the true meanings of some festivals is lost or people don't think about it and just use it as an excuse to spend money and to go to parties. A lot of the time is spent under pressure as a lot of hard work goes into preparing everything for the festival. This is not how it should be. Celebration should be a time of peace and goodwill.

The celebrations of all religions should be as big and great as they can as it is a celebration of something wonderful that's happened. This is what some people believe. A lot of discrimination takes place and, although everyone thinks that they are not prejudiced, why is it that Christmas is a very public event – everyone knows about it, lights and decorations go up in shops – whereas you don't know or are not aware of festivals such as Divali and Passover.

Basically, everyone celebrates festivals, whether they know why or what happened. Is this right?

A festival is a time for rejoicing, a time to remember, an aspect of a religion, happy or sad. It gets people together to help them worship as a whole. It is a time for families and friends to relate

*cont.*

to each other. The world is always so busy that people don't have time to relax with families and friends. A festival helps them do that.

Different types of presents and food help people to remember the religion (e.g. Easter eggs – new life through Jesus' death; Passover – the order of food symbolizing the Jews' plight and freedom).

Unfortunately, with the fun and excitement comes hassle and expense. If special food has to be eaten, this has to be bought and cooked. For the time of a festival, people's lives can be made chaos. It is not always easy to celebrate a religious festival in a non-religious society. For example, the food or clothes, even times, needed may not be available. Fasting could be difficult for children at school or adults at work when colleagues or friends are eating.

I don't think it's appropriate for non-religious people to celebrate the festivals if they don't understand the meaning behind them fully. It's not fair for them to treat them as an excuse for a party.

Festivals are important to the followers of religion as they are the time for remembering events that happened to change the religion's history.

If those events had not happened then the way our world runs could be completely different.

Festivals are not just times for having parties and having a good time. They should be for celebrating important things and only things with a religious significance.

If the reason for celebrating festivals is unknown then there is no point.

We can have a good time if we know and believe that what we are celebrating is important and valuable.

## GROUP 5

**Group Description**
Year 11, GCSE Religious Studies set

**Theme**
Personal Attitudes to Faith

**Teaching Objectives**
To provide opportunities for students to develop general skills in research and specific skills in handling and interpreting evidence of religious expression

**Time Allowed**
Overnight

**Resources Used**
All of the first five Students' Books in the *Faith and Commitment* series

ACTIVITY

Individually, students chose one interviewee from one *Faith and Commitment* book, all of whose interview extracts they read. They then wrote up what they had found out about their interviewee's attitude towards and involvement in their faith.

### SAMPLES OF STUDENTS' WORK

I chose to look at the interviews of Edna M [*Committed to Judaism: A Jewish Community*].

I read the section on Where I Belong. I learnt that one of the most important things to Edna is her family and making sure the children are brought up in a traditional Jewish way.

Edna feels strongly about being over-judgemental of people and not doing things she can't give everything she's got to.

The festivals Edna likes most are Shavuot, Pesach and Shabbat. The reasons for these are different. She likes Shavuot because it is relaxing and religiously uplifting. She likes Pesach because it is satisfying after all the hard work she puts in. But she likes the Shabbat because it is just a day out of the week to relax and spend time with her family and friends. Edna feels some of the dos and don'ts are complicated and that what matters most is sticking to the basics of religion and leading a full life.

*cont.*

## SAMPLES OF STUDENTS' WORK                              *cont.*

Out of most of what I read I realized that children are one of the most important things to Edna and that they have helped to bring out the best in her faith.

I've noticed in what I read that Edna tries to relate her beliefs to everyday life.

I feel that Edna feels proud of being Jewish but in a way feels responsible for events that happen. I feel she doesn't like or understand the way Jews are treated differently but she has come to terms with it.

---

Ray [*Committed to Christianity: A Pentecostal Community*] was once in the Royal Navy, but now he works in London. He married a girl called Desreen over a year ago.

He helps with a youth club which is attached to the church but is not a church organization. Everyone is invited to the youth club and is shown what the church has to offer. Ray believes that you should reach out to people without punching the Bible, which tends to put people off.

Ray also attends a Bible class. He is very committed to helping non-Christians and showing them what Christianity is all about. He gives up a great deal of his spare time to do this. Ray feels very strongly that a church should be filled with emotion and feeling. He says God should be given the highest honour and glory. He also states that Christians should do more to help the poor and needy, just like Jesus did. Ray would perhaps like to be a deacon one day.

Comment: Ray is very devoted to the Christian faith and obviously loves his God a great deal. He gives up much of his spare time to helping others. He is a true Christian.

## GROUP 6

**Group Description**
(A) Year 12, A-level Religious Studies set
(B) Year 13, A-level Religious Studies set

**Theme**
A Special Moment

**Teaching Objectives**
To investigate important experiences and their relationship to religious expression

**Time Allowed**
One forty-minute session with each group

**Resources Used**
Music cassette
*Committed to Christianity: An Anglican Community*, pages 31 to 36
*Committed to Christianity: A Pentecostal Community*, pages 32 to 38
*Committed to Christianity: A Roman Catholic Community*, pages 32 to 39
*Committed to Hinduism: A Hindu Community*, pages 34 to 38
*Committed to Judaism: A Jewish Community*, pages 34 to 37

ACTIVITY: GROUPS A AND B

*Teacher* played group a piece of music and explained why it was special to her.

*Group and teacher* discussed what a 'special moment' might involve. Ideas that came up included: something unforgettable, a turning-point, a decision, marking an occasion, a re-evaluation, a change of mind.

*Individually*, students wrote about a moment that was special to them. Some moments were then shared.

*In small groups*, students read 'A Special Moment' interview extracts from the five *Faith and Commitment* books and began discussing them in terms of differences in type of experience – personal, private, communal, shared.

*Group and teacher* considered why people often want to express their special monents. Ideas that came up included: enriching one's experience of life, providing memories (good and bad), awakening emotions, discovering or rediscovering one's inner self.

*Students* read to the rest of the group a special moment from the *Faith and Commitment* books of their choosing.

*Discussion* went on to consider whether having a faith makes any difference to a person's susceptibility to experiencing special moments. Students concluded that spirituality in any form is an important factor.

## ACTIVITY: GROUP B ONLY

*Group and teacher* went on to think about Judaism in particular. Students were particularly struck by insights into what it means to be one of the Chosen People. It was generally agreed that descriptions such as Sandy's special moment at candle-lighting time and Jeffrey's sighting of Mount Carmel on his way to Israel made sense of the belief behind the ritual, practice and shared religious heritage of Judaism.

## TEACHER'S COMMENTS

It was a privilege to share my own experiences and the experiences described in the books with students. There was the additional reward of having the lessons turned into a special moment in their own right.

---

**EXTRACTS FROM STUDENTS' WORK**

Christmas Eve will always make me think of my Gran, as I went to see her in hospital and I knew it would be the very last time. I don't know what made me so sure. I was the last person to visit her, as she died a few hours later. At the time, I was terribly upset, but now, talking about special moments today, I think that seeing her that night was one of mine.

Landscapes in Ireland. So big. Felt insignificant but also part of it. If I went back, I don't think it would be the same.

I can remember one morning waking up and I felt really at peace with everything. It only lasted a few seconds or maybe minutes. It's really inexplicable and I've never had it again.

The band had recently played in a school assembly. They were a Christian rock band. When we were at the YMCA, they said a prayer for us all and I felt an overpowering sense of warmth and love. This feeling is very hard to describe but I will never forget it. I felt another presence in the room and the feeling of hope, love and security surrounded me.

I think that anyone who says they have never felt a special moment have most probably denied themselves the recognition of what they have felt. They have denied themselves a wonderful feeling or sensation most probably because they

*cont.*

## EXTRACTS FROM STUDENTS' WORK                          *cont.*

don't feel anything for religion. Accepting something like this is like accepting religion.

It can be very personal to me, and special, but sharing a moment with others makes it lose its value somewhat, as I feel it may seem silly to them.

Special moments do not have to be religion-based. Most involve someone or something else to make them special moments.

When praying for something or someone, I get a special feeling that God will actually do it.

Sitting in my room on my own with music with the lights out and lit candles, this is a special moment. Being by myself.

A special moment for me was when I left my old school because we were boarders so were very close, like sisters. In our last assembly together, we sang our favourite hymn. That will always be my favourite.

Everyone has different special moments, which can occur under different circumstances. They are very important to that person and remain with them forever. In some cases, after experiencing that special moment, it seems as if everything has changed, that you can start afresh. It can sometimes be thought of as a turning-point in your life.

Thank you. I enjoyed the lesson. It is very appropriate for me at the moment, for I am going through a very special time, although it is very sad ... I've had many special moments and now I'll spend the rest of the day thinking of them!

■ Each Students' Book in the *Faith and Commitment* series has three systems of internal organization:

- **Thematic sections** entitled:

  **About Me**
  **Where I Belong**
  **What I Feel Strongly About**
  **My Favourite Festival**
  **A Special Moment**
  **Words That Mean a Lot to Me**
  **Things I Find Challenging**

  These provided the explicit framework for our development of the books, for the questions we asked and the answers which people gave us during interviews. Everyone who participated in the project was aware of these terms of reference. Their responses acknowledge the implications of the terms we used and interpret them knowingly.

- **Index by key words** Indexes were produced during the final editorial stage of production after all interview extracts had been selected by us and shown to the communities. Each index aims to achieve an objective reference to content via key words. To provide consistency across the series, the key words include a spine of generic terms, such as 'priest', which are used in addition to the specific term a community might use, such as 'vicar' or 'pujari'.

- **Interviewee colour-coding** All interview extracts are credited to interviewees by name. Usually, just a forename is given, or when two or more members of the same family were interviewed, a forename plus the initial of their surname. To help users of the books identify specific interviewees' contributions, a personalized colour-coding is established when each interviewee's first contribution to a book appears, in the opening section, 'About Me'. This colour-coding is repeated in the presentation of further contributions.

In addition, the tables which follow provide:

- **Analysis by teaching/learning focus** This uses seventeen headings to analyse the interview content in a more technical way. The headings refer to concepts which are relevant to meeting the current requirements of teaching and learning in RE and developing the spiritual, moral, social and cultural awareness of students:

  **Culture**
  **Morality: Personal**
  **Morality: Social**
  **Religious Expression: Community**
  **Religious Expression: Festivals**
  **Religious Expression: Laws and Duties**
  **Religious Expression: Prayer, Praise and Worship**
  **Religious Expression: Rites of Passage**

Religious Expression: Roles
Religious Expression: Sacred Books
Religious Expression: Social Action
Religious Expression: Symbols, Special Actions and Artefacts
Society: Family
Society: Pressures
Spirituality: Ideas of God
Spirituality: Personal Experiences
Spirituality: Personal Faith

In each entry under these headings, a possible teaching/learning focus contained in an interview extract is summarized by a quotation taken from that extract. If a quotation indicates more than one focus, it is listed more than once. Similarly, if an interview extract provides several different teaching/learning focuses, more than one quotation is listed. Every extract is represented at least once. However, the listing is not exhaustive nor intended to be a substitute for exploring and getting to know the material first-hand.

The tabular format of this analysis should not be used as a basis for making comparisons between denominations or religions. Interviewees were not asked questions according to the headings listed in these tables, and any comparative conclusions drawn from the presence, absence or nature of the responses analysed may be of doubtful validity.

- **List of illustrations** All religious items shown are listed. Where the item has a special personal significance in addition to its religious one, this is explained.

In addition, further details about some personal photos and other items are given where these are not clear from the context or where more information is available.

## AN ANGLICAN COMMUNITY

## RELIGIOUS EXPRESSION: SYMBOLS, SPECIAL ACTIONS AND ARTEFACTS

| | |
|---|---|
| I belong where I can be quiet. | 16 |
| I carry ... the incense-holder. | 24 |
| 'I've washed your feet. You must wash one another's.' | 24 |
| We do a dawn Eucharist on Easter Sunday morning. It's pitch black except for the paschal candle. | 25 |
| A watch is kept throughout the night until the service for Good Friday starts. | 26 |
| Music in the service can very much change how I'm feeling. So can lack of music. | 28 |
| In the depths of winter, in the middle of the night, the church is filled with light, and joy, and singing. | 30 |
| I love anything that involves the lighting of candles. | 37 |

## SOCIETY: FAMILY

| | |
|---|---|
| I used to be a teacher but gave up my job to have Rowan. | 6 |
| I think it's easy to lose your identity as a mother. | 10 |
| I look back and think I had an above averagely miserable childhood. | 12 |
| I feel very strongly about family values. | 20 |

## SOCIETY: PRESSURES

| | |
|---|---|
| My job's taking up far too many hours a week. | 7 |
| I'm confronted with a huge pile of ironing and a baby to feed. Then I think, 'Ah, yes, but should I go and read the Bible for half and hour?' | 46 |
| Finding a balance between working life and family life and religious and church activity. I find that very difficult. | 47 |

## SPIRITUALITY: IDEAS OF GOD

| | |
|---|---|
| The God I want to believe in is a God who's with us in our suffering and is as crucified by it as we are. | 33 |
| I felt God had taken hold of the situation. | 39 |
| Magic in the end you can explain ... but a mystery gets bigger the more you examine it. | 40 |
| 'Lord of all hopefulness'. I love the idea behind it – God being with you through the day and also through your life. | 42 |
| 'Lord of the dance' | 43 |
| I believe we've been given freedom by a God who very much wants us to 'grow up', if you like, just like a parent. | 44 |

## SPIRITUALITY: PERSONAL EXPERIENCES

| | |
|---|---|
| Suddenly the little chapel seemed to be flooded with light. | 31 |
| I look back to moments in my life when I was aware of a deep sense of utter helplessness and yet of being in the right place. | 32 |
| I think the confirmation was quite a turning-point for me. Late twenties is relatively late for people to be confirmed. | 34 |
| Our marriage was really special. | 35 |
| When Moira walked down the aisle, it was the first time she'd walked without crutches. | 35 |
| 'See what God has given you.' And I saw that what he'd given me was Eleanor, our handicapped daughter. | 35 |
| There was this wretched hymn I couldn't get out of my mind. | 36 |

## SPIRITUALITY: PERSONAL FAITH

| | |
|---|---|
| I became a member of the Third Order of St Francis. I felt it was a very strong vocation. | 8 |
| I don't know where my faith comes from. | 11 |
| [Faith is] a bit like a sense of humour. It's something that's given. | 12 |
| I'd find it hard to commit myself completely to any one faith. | 17 |
| I was brought up believing [in Christianity]. | 19 |
| I feel strongly about the fact that I have a faith. | 22 |
| My idea of religion is that it's personal. You're the first person I've ever talked to about religion. | 22 |
| I find Christianity extremely difficult to unravel. | 47 |

## A PENTECOSTAL COMMUNITY

## RELIGIOUS EXPRESSION: ROLES

| | |
|---|---|
| I'm assistant catering officer for the church. | 7 |
| I'm a minister with the New Testament Assembly. | 10 |
| I'm currently one of the Young People's Leaders within the church. | 13 |
| On Fridays I help out with the Youth Group. | 14 |
| I'm just one of the congregation. But there might be more for me to do in future years. That's a challenge. | 47 |

## RELIGIOUS EXPRESSION: SACRED BOOKS

| | |
|---|---|
| We teach the word of God, we preach it. But it's the personal relationship with God that's important. | 26 |
| If you can hear God from within, he can minister to you. There are times when God will give me passages from the Bible. | 42 |

## RELIGIOUS EXPRESSION: SOCIAL ACTION

| | |
|---|---|
| When I look at the mission of Christ, Christ was a street person. | 22 |
| Jesus went out and did things. He didn't stay in a church preaching. | 27 |
| What I find difficult about being a Christian is showing that you're a Christian. | 46 |
| Our church goes out into the community and talks to people. | 46 |

## RELIGIOUS EXPRESSION: SYMBOLS, SPECIAL ACTIONS AND ARTEFACTS

| | |
|---|---|
| I had to go down into the water – total immersion. | 32 |
| People in this community will fast quite often … It's a sacrifice. | 37 |

## SOCIETY: FAMILY

| | |
|---|---|
| I come from a church family. | 6 |
| I've fostered five children already. | 7 |
| My parents, grandparents and so forth were Christian. | 8 |
| My family's quite closely knit and I thank God for the love I've had. | 12 |
| I do think your family sows the seeds of what you believe. | 16 |
| I know how God has treated us … I want that to be passed on to my children. | 23 |

## SOCIETY: PRESSURES

| | |
|---|---|
| As a teenager, I thought church life, especially in the Pentecostal world, was very strict. I wanted to go out, enjoy myself with friends. | 17 |
| I'll go to college and friends there will invite me to parties. | 33 |
| I thought, 'There's nothing hotter than me, man. I can make it!' | 36 |

## SPIRITUALITY: IDEAS OF GOD

| | |
|---|---|
| I view God basically as my father … He won't let anything happen to me. | 8 |
| There's always a voice there to speak to me, the voice of Christ. | 15 |
| God is unique – in the relationship I have with him, in the way he directs my life. | 20 |
| I know what God can do. | 25 |
| I praise God that I did receive the Holy Spirit. Now he's with me all the time. | 35 |
| God has always made me feel special. | 42 |
| 'The Lord is my light and my salvation. Whom shall I fear?' | 42 |

## SPIRITUALITY: PERSONAL EXPERIENCES

| | |
|---|---|
| Going to college was a step of faith for me. If I hadn't gone ahead, I wouldn't have known how God worked things out. | 21 |
| There was my college exam. I hadn't studied. | 25 |
| One day I was washing my car and I just stood, searching my soul. | 32 |
| The Holy Spirit came down and I felt enlightened, like I was floating, just not there. | 34 |
| I put it down to God, definitely. I don't think it's possible to explain. | 35 |
| All I saw was a sort of silhouette. I was beginning to wonder myself whether I was going mad. | 36 |
| God knew my desire was to get into the Probation Service. | 38 |

## SPIRITUALITY: PERSONAL FAITH

| | |
|---|---|
| Slowly I became an unbeliever, an atheist. | 11 |
| It's more than saying I serve God. It's a kind of assurance. It's very, very personal. | 20 |

## A ROMAN CATHOLIC COMMUNITY

### MORALITY: PERSONAL

| | |
|---|---|
| I try to live the way Christ intended. I don't always succeed, but I'm trying. | 15 |
| I feel strongly about family. | 21 |
| I feel strongly about the sanctity of life and about allowing people to have dignity. | 23 |
| I think really the baseline is that my Christianity matters to me ... It's what I try to live out day to day. | 24 |
| I've got a lot of things coming up now, challenging things, especially drugs. | 37 |
| 'Lord, make me an instrument of your peace.' | 43 |
| I like the word 'peace'. | 43 |
| You've got to be nice to everybody. | 44 |

### MORALITY: SOCIAL

| | |
|---|---|
| I feel strongly about euthanasia. | 22 |
| I think abortion's awful. | 22 |
| I don't like seeing those kids in Romania. | 23 |

### RELIGIOUS EXPRESSION: COMMUNITY

| | |
|---|---|
| People who aren't Catholic don't think that I'm odd. They just accept me, really, for who I am. | 8 |
| My mum expects me to go to church. | 10 |
| The Emmaus Family of Prayer is a local group involving about two hundred people in different ways. | 14 |
| We're a big community. Very together. | 16 |
| When I think of being a Catholic, I think of a big community. | 16 |
| I don't think I'm labelled as belonging to a certain place ... I can worship quite happily anywhere. | 16 |
| There'd have been about forty people in the room. I turned up and thought, 'There's something good happening here.' | 17 |
| I've been brought up and live in the Agape Community ... It was two families trying to live a more community-based life. | 20 |
| What's good about being a Christian is that there's a support network. | 44 |

### RELIGIOUS EXPRESSION: FESTIVALS

| | |
|---|---|
| If there was no other celebration in the entire year, the one you'd be left with would be the Easter Vigil. | 27 |
| The Easter Vigil is the first Mass, *the* celebration, of Easter. | 28 |
| Growing up on a farm ... the whole idea of re-creation and new life and resurrection is something that's special to me, and I'd associate that with Easter. | 29 |
| Easter ... gives you a chance to start all over again. | 29 |
| I like Christmas because there's just something in the air. | 30 |
| I think it's good we celebrate Christmas. And it shows, doesn't it. | 30 |
| Christmas is a family celebration. | 31 |
| Everyone seems to make a point of getting together at Christmas. | 31 |

### RELIGIOUS EXPRESSION: PRAYER, PRAISE AND WORSHIP

| | |
|---|---|
| I don't feel I'm labelled as belonging to a certain place ... I can worship quite happily anywhere. | 16 |
| There are differences between generations of Catholics and this is leading to differences in styles of worship and between churches. | 18 |
| Once, when we were camping in Sweden, I found out that the nearest Catholic church was in Norway! We went. | 19 |
| Sometimes, when I'm praying, I'll get a sense – like of family and belonging. | 20 |
| Prayer makes you feel that you can do something about something. | 33 |
| I don't have one special prayer. I tend to use my own words and make prayers up. | 43 |

### RELIGIOUS EXPRESSION: RITES OF PASSAGE

| | |
|---|---|
| People were asking me when I was going to be ordained a priest. I kept telling them, 'Never!' | 12 |
| I'd had quite a deep change in my spirituality, in my faith. You could call it a conversion. | 17 |
| [During the Easter Vigil] we renew the promises made at our baptism. | 26 |
| I really enjoyed my First Communion. | 35 |
| Confirmation was a special moment for me. | 37 |
| 'Death is nothing at all.' | 40 |

### RELIGIOUS EXPRESSION: ROLES

| | |
|---|---|
| I've been involved fairly heavily in voluntary youth work. | 11 |
| I'm a priest in the Catholic church. | 12 |
| I work for the Emmaus Family of Prayer group as a full-time youth worker. | 14 |

## A HINDU COMMUNITY

## RELIGIOUS EXPRESSION: RITES OF PASSAGE

## RELIGIOUS EXPRESSION: ROLES

## RELIGIOUS EXPRESSION: SACRED BOOKS

## RELIGIOUS EXPRESSION: SYMBOLS, SPECIAL ACTIONS AND ARTEFACTS

## SOCIETY: FAMILY

## SOCIETY: PRESSURES

## SPIRITUALITY: IDEAS OF GOD

## SPIRITUALITY: PERSONAL EXPERIENCES

## SPIRITUALITY: PERSONAL FAITH

## A JEWISH COMMUNITY

### CULTURE

### MORALITY: PERSONAL

### MORALITY: SOCIAL

### RELIGIOUS EXPRESSION: COMMUNITY

### RELIGIOUS EXPRESSION: FESTIVALS

### RELIGIOUS EXPRESSION: LAWS AND DUTIES

## RELIGIOUS EXPRESSION: PRAYER, PRAISE AND WORSHIP

## RELIGIOUS EXPRESSION: RITES OF PASSAGE

## RELIGIOUS EXPRESSION: ROLES

## RELIGIOUS EXPRESSION: SACRED BOOKS

## RELIGIOUS EXPRESSION: SYMBOLS, SPECIAL ACTIONS AND ARTEFACTS

## SOCIETY: FAMILY

## SOCIETY: PRESSURES

## SPIRITUALITY: IDEAS OF GOD

cont.

## SPIRITUALITY: PERSONAL EXPERIENCES

## SPIRITUALITY: PERSONAL FAITH

# LIST OF ILLUSTRATIONS

## A ROMAN CATHOLIC COMMUNITY

### RELIGIOUS ITEMS

### PERSONAL ITEMS

### PERSONAL ITEMS  cont.

## A HINDU COMMUNITY

### RELIGIOUS ITEMS

### PERSONAL ITEMS

## RELIGIOUS ITEMS

## PERSONAL ITEMS

*Note* The Torah scroll featured here is a facsimile which has not been prepared for ritual use. It is one of a range of religious artefacts selected as suitable for classroom use available for purchase from: Articles of Faith Ltd, Bury Business Centre, Kay Street, BURY BL9 6BU.

# NOTES